The Animals of White Cows Farm

Heather Peck

Published in 2024 by Ormesby Publishing

Ormesby St Margaret

Norfolk

www.ormesbypublishing.co.uk

British Library Cataloguing in Publication Data

A CIP catalogue record for this book is available from the British Library.

Page design and typesetting by Ormesby Publishing

ACKNOWLEDGMENTS

Many thanks again to my beta reader Gary Westlake for his constructive criticism and extremely helpful comments. This book is all the better for your help.

Thanks also to the talented Rebecca Holt for the illustrations

This book is dedicated to the pupils of Ormesby School
in fulfilment of a promise I made them
on World Book Day 2024

CONTENTS

Foreword

A farm is a magical place. It has so many different dimensions, Dr Who would be jealous.

It produces food for humans and many other animals, seen and unseen.

It provides a living space for many families: some big, some so small you can only see them with a microscope.

Millions of babies are born there every year; some speak, some baa or moo, cheep or squawk; some run, some crawl, some swim. Many can fly.

It soaks up rain, bathes in sunlight, and its soil is the basis for all life.

And the most magical thing of all – every animal on the farm has its own place. They all fit together like the pieces of a jigsaw. Even the humans.

This is the story of one of those magical places.

And of the lives of some of its animals.

Introducing White Cows Farm

The first thing you need to know about White Cows Farm is that there are lots of animals, but none of them are white cows. The second thing you need to know is that you will find it in Norfolk; that wonderful county in the East of England, where the lakes are called Broads, the beaches are wide, and the skies stretch from horizon to horizon with no mountains to get in the way. White Cows Farm lies on land between the Broads and the sea. Its soil is sandy, and the weather is often dry.

Marigold the house cow is gold and white. Her mum was a Jersey cow, and that's where the gold came from. It also makes her milk very rich and creamy. Her dad was a Friesian, and that's where the white came from, especially the white stripe down her nose that makes her eyes cross if she tries to look at it for too long. Because her dad was a Friesian, she also gives lots and lots of milk.

Besides Marigold there are some more golden-brown cows in the fields. These are not milked by Farmer Fred like Marigold but have lots of pretty brown calves with them. Their job is to look after their calves until they grow up.

Farmer Fred likes to think he's in charge of the farm. His father farmed at White Cows, and *his* father before him. For all Fred knows, his family have farmed that patch of land all the way back to the Saxons. Their blood and sweat are in the soil. Their bodies are in the churchyard. The farm animals at White Cows look the way they do, because of choices Farmer Fred's family has made over many, many years. But Fred isn't really in charge. He serves the farm, and the farm serves him. If *anything* is in charge, it's the weather. If *anyone* is in charge, it's probably Gertie Goose.

But let's get back to meeting some of the animals. There are sheep in the long fields at the top of the farm, and some pigs in the field near the farmhouse; and of course, there are Gertie Goose and her friends - the hens, and Scratchy Patch - the spaniel, all living in the barn and the house. At least, Patch lives in the house. The hens and Gertie were shooed out if they sneaked in.

Of course, not all the animals are as big as Marigold, nor even as big as the sheep. Take Needles the hedgehog, for example. Needles lives in a big, warm pile of dead leaves in the orchard that Farmer Fred piled up in the autumn. She went to bed there when the weather grew cold and slept all through the snowy days and the gales and hail. Now it is the Spring, she has woken up and as the days grow longer and warmer, she has her babies; four fine hoglets. When they were born all their spines were soft and they had no protection at all from enemies, so she kept them safely in her nest and fed them on her milk. She went out alone at night to find food: fine juicy slugs on the garden plants and leatherjackets hidden in the lawn. If Farmer Fred saw her at night, he always said *'thank you'* to her, for clearing up the pests from his garden. Sometimes he gave her some of Patch's meaty dog food.

Now it's March, the hoglets spines have hardened and Needles can bring her family out into the garden in the evening, to show them what is good to eat. Prickles and Sharpy think the slugs are great, while Thorny and Bristles are more interested in the pond and the insects popping up to the surface. In actual fact, there are two ponds. One is big and has broad, gently sloping, muddy banks. This is Gertie's pond, and the hedgehogs daren't go there. Gertie is so loud, so talkative and so BOSSY, that most animals that have any choice stay out of her way. The second pond is much smaller and more decorative. It's surrounded by stone flags and has yellow iris flowering at one end as well as waterlilies bobbing about in the middle. Sometimes, if the hoglets watch carefully, they will see a big fat carp poke its nose up from under a lily pad and snatch a mayfly with a big gulp. And hidden in amongst the iris stems they will often find the balls of jelly with black dots in the middle that are frogspawn. Needles doesn't like her children messing about by the pond. But Bristles and Thorny are very fond of frogspawn, very fond indeed.

On this chilly evening, the whole family is out hunting for their supper. There are a few slugs about, but the soil is still cold, so the worms have gone deep. The hoglets have spread out to dig in the flowerbeds, and two of them are thinking about the possibility of frogspawn in the pond.

'Keep clear of the pond,' Needles told them again and again, worried about trying to keep track of them all. Bristles and Thorny paid no attention and were moving closer to the frogspawn, hoping that she wouldn't notice. Needles took her eye off them for just one minute and plop, Bristles had fallen in and was swimming around. The pond edge was steep, and he couldn't get out! Every time he tried, he slipped back in; and he was getting very tired.

'Mum!' he tried to shout, but all that came out was a wet gurgle.

'Mum!' shouted Thorny, and this time Needles heard. She dashed over to the pond and saw the problem straight away.

'Bristles,' she called, 'come to me.' Bristles heard and swam once more across the pond with his very last strength. There was a ramp which Farmer Fred had thoughtfully put into the pond just for hedgehogs! Bristles climbed on to the ramp and staggered off on to the grass.

'Oh Mum!' was all he could say.

After a bit of a rest, Needles and her family made their way back to the pile of leaves in the orchard. They passed Marigold grazing quietly in the moonlight and saw a rat running by the hedge. Then a silent shadow sailed overhead, cutting out the moon just for a moment as it went by.

'Quick!' shouted Needles, her voice a bit muffled because her nose was next to her tail. 'Curl!' All the hoglets curled up tight and their new stiff spines stuck out all round. Hoot, the barn owl, sailed on by to look for easier prey, and the hoglets all relaxed. Needles led them back to their nest.

'Remember,' she said, as they went to sleep just as dawn was breaking. 'Danger can come from above as well as below, and if you're in a pond, look for a ramp!' The hoglets didn't take much notice as they were very tired, but Needles would make sure they practiced rolling up every day after that. She liked Hoot, but her babies were not going to be his supper!

The Robin's Tale

Robin was born one cold morning early in March. Or, to be more accurate, he hatched himself. When he met his mother later that day, he took her to task about the lack of help. He thought it a little hard that he had to break out of his shell all on his own, with no help from anyone. It had been hard work and took a lot of battering with the egg tooth on the end of his baby beak, and lots of turning round and round and trying again. Even when he made the first hole and could peer out at the world with his bright little eye, still no-one helped. He just had to keep going, pecking and battering and pushing, until his tiny 2 cm shell fell apart and there he was.

Hatched! Or born, if you prefer!

He found himself in a grassy nest with 4 other robin chicks. The warm pile of moss, grass and fluff was all inside an old kettle pushed into the middle of a tall hedge. Cold fresh air came down the spout and his mother was sitting on the rim. She may have been a bit slow in the helping-with-hatching department, but she was a cracker at providing breakfast. Barely had Robin got his beak open than a small insect was pushed in. Very tasty it was too. His brothers and sisters got insects as well, and then they settled down together in the middle of the nest, feathers fluffed out for warmth.

A few days later, everything changed. Instead of bringing the insects to the open beaks, Mum sat on the rim and waved one encouragingly. All the little robins responded by waving their beaks, equally encouragingly, but this time, nothing went in. Mum hopped off the kettle and out into the hedge. Bother! Open beaks inside, insect outside, and it was clear that the Mum who had been pretty useless at hatching was now deteriorating sharply on the insect front too. Sighing heavily, Robin followed the insect and was rewarded with a meal.

But now he was out of the nest and in the hedge. Hedges, he discovered, were very well designed for perching. They have lots of footholds, and you can hop down to the ground in easy steps. He hopped on down, and Mum rewarded him with another meal. Then she showed him where the meal came from. This was really exciting, and he discovered it was a lot of fun scratching in the soft ground under the hedge. What he hadn't quite realized was that he would never see the old kettle again. Chick-hood was over, and he didn't belong in the nest anymore. He would have to find his own roost and his own insects from here on.

Things were about to get a lot tougher. One day he was peacefully scratching around for insects and worms, when he was viciously attacked from above by his own father!

'Get out, get out,' his father hissed, and pecked hard at Robin's back. 'There is only room for one Robin in this garden, and that robin is me! Get out. Get out.' What would have happened next is anyone's guess, but luckily Robin got his new wings to work just in time, and rather clumsily fluttered away over the hedge with the kettle and through a small wood.

Quite out of breath and feeling very sore, he stopped for a rest on a small tree in a farmhouse garden. He looked around nervously. He could see a blackbird singing sweetly in another tree, but it didn't seem to mind him being there. He could see a squirrel stealing nuts out of a bird feeder, but the squirrel didn't seem to mind him either. Then he saw a cat, but the cat was the other side a tall fence and didn't seem to be coming his way. He started to relax, and to think about his next insect. Over in the corner, he saw a patch of ground which had been turned over ready for planting potatoes. It was dark and soft, moist and full of worms and insects. He flew over and started scratching.

First, he found a worm, and then a leatherjacket. The day that had started so badly was starting to look up. He had just collared another leatherjacket when Farmer Fred came out of the kitchen with a mug of tea and sat on a bench by the potato patch. They eyed each other. Robin was wary but knew he could fly away quickly if the man made a grab. Fred was just pleased to see Robin eating all his garden pests and didn't want to scare him away. So he drank his tea quietly and didn't make any sudden moves.

'I like this garden,' thought Robin. *'I like the insects, and the man seems quiet and well behaved. There isn't another robin to threaten me,'* (he thought of his father and shuddered). *'All that's lacking is a kettle.'*

He did a circuit of the garden to see what else was there (and just to check again for a kettle). There was a small fountain in a pond that would provide water. There were some gnats rising from the pond too, and they went the same way as the leatherjackets. There were paths, and lawns and flowerbeds with lots of loose earth. There were some bird feeders full of peanuts (much too big for a Robin) and a house with creepers growing on it. There were lots of insects in the creepers too! There was a barn nearby, fields and a yard full of straw and mud. But no kettle.

Just as he had to give up on the kettle, he noticed something else. Hanging on the wall of the house were two brooms, a small shovel and two watering cans. One of the watering cans was hanging right way up and had water in it. The other was hanging upside down near the creeper, and it was dry.

'Well, it's not a kettle,' said Robin, 'but it's nearly as good as a kettle.' He had a look inside and a little poke around. 'Actually,' he said, his voice muffled and echoing, 'it is very like a kettle. It has a handle and a spout just the same. It might do......'

Just to test it, he flew to the fence where some sheep had rubbed on the wire and left some wool behind. He picked up the wool and carried it to the watering can, and put it in. Regarding it with his head on one side he thought a little, then fetched some moss. Some dry grass followed, some straw, then some more wool. A nest was taking shape. Farmer Fred saw all the work going on and smiled to himself, making a mental note that he would need a new watering can. The old one had obviously been requisitioned as Robin accommodation.

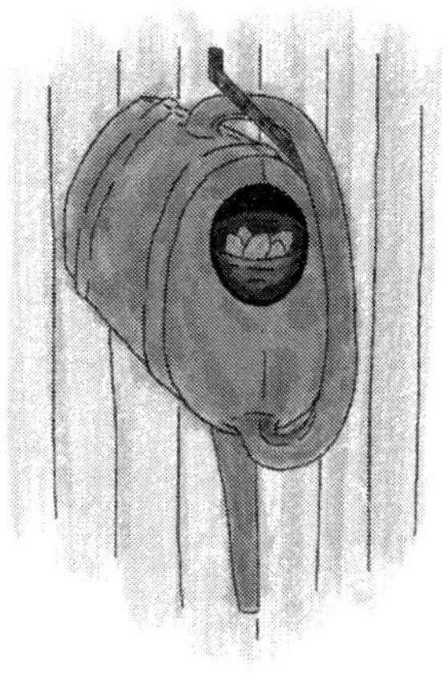

By the summer, there were 5 small creamy eggs in the old watering can, and the cycle of robin life was beginning over again.

Spring, Eostre the Hare, and Trouble

Spring at White Cows Farm always meant lambs.

'Lambs, lambs and more lambs,' muttered Marigold the House Cow, as she enjoyed a few moments in the sun one April morning. Had she known it, those were almost exactly Farmer Fred's words when he got up that morning.

'You know I love lambing,' he had said to Mrs Fred that morning, 'but by April I've just about had enough of staying up all night and feeding pet lambs.'

'You should teach Patch to do it,' she had said, 'like that dog in the papers.'

'Oh yes,' said Fred, 'I should coco!'

'So should I,' thought Patch and slunk away in a hurry. She liked her warm basket at night and had no wish to spend hours feeding those bouncy pet lambs.

But that April morning, as Marigold had noticed, the sun was shining, the lambs were all playing mad games up and down the field, and the ewes were grazing peacefully. Farmer Fred did his normal walk round at lunchtime, and all was well. He heaved a sigh of relief as he went in for his tea. Patch looked after him but decided to go for a wander on her own.

The first field she reached, she wriggled under the 5-bar gate and joined Marigold who was grazing the short spring grass.

'Sssh,' said Marigold, indistinctly through a mouthful of cud. 'Look over there,' and she pointed with a toss of her nose.

Patch looked, and there were two hares, jumping and prancing and, as Patch watched, one of them gave the other a resounding box on the ear.

'Wow,' said Patch, 'I wouldn't like to pick a fight with him!'

'That's not the him,' said Marigold. 'That's the her. The him is the one who has just run off. Meet my friend Ēostre.'

'That's a funny name,' remarked Patch. 'I haven't heard that before.'

'It's the old name for the Spring festival,' replied Marigold. 'We call it Easter now, which sounds almost the same but is spelt differently.'

Patch didn't bother a lot about spelling, so she took no notice. The big hare named Ēostre was looking over at Marigold but didn't come any closer. She could smell Patch and she didn't trust dogs, so she stared a little, then drummed her feet on the ground to warn other hares around that there was a predator about.

Marigold started to move towards Ēostre. She knew the hare didn't mind cows and they were old friends. Patch would have followed, but she had just caught a whiff of a very interesting smell. She put her nose in the air and followed it across the field, down the lane and round the corner. There she stopped dead. Now she knew what the smell was! It was a mixture of two strange men, a strange dog, and the oily smell of a rather elderly van. Patch didn't like the smell of the van, or the men, and the dog that was getting out of the van was even worse. Ēostre had vanished and Marigold could just see her in the distance, galloping up the field and shouting warnings. The van was pulled up on the verge near the field gate and as Patch watched, the dog started into the field. The sheep, alert to an unknown dog, started to move together, with their lambs on the inside of the flock. The noise of their bleating rose in the sleepy afternoon air.

In an instant, Patch whipped round and dashed back to the farmyard. There was no time to be lost, and she went into action to alert the White Cows Farm Neighbourhood Watch. First, she woke Gertie the Goose from her afternoon nap and she, with all her goslings, started making a tremendous racket. Next, she pushed the latch up on the barn. In moments, all the golden cows and their calves were out of the barn, down the road and, joined by Marigold, were milling around the scruffy van. The two men, saying a lot of rude words, found their every move was stopped by a big, bony cow bum. Marigold and her friends knew full well that if their heads were out of reach, there wasn't much a human or dog could do with a tight packed row of cow bums.

Finally, Patch fetched Farmer Fred who, after a moments panic, could only laugh at the would-be sheep rustlers, deafened by geese and trapped by cows.

By the time the police arrived, the furious sheep rustlers and their van were covered in cow dung and one of them was hopping about, after Marigold, quite deliberately, stood on his foot. The police confiscated the van and took the men and the dog away. Farmer Fred patted Patch.

'Well done old girl,' he said. 'Only one problem. Who's going to get all these cows back to the barn?' Patch sat down and scratched hard. 'Nothing to do with her,' she thought, and noticed that, in the distance, Ēostre was boxing another set of ears. All was well again.

A Spring Hatch

One late Spring morning, when the winds were warm, Marigold the house cow was interested to see something new happening in the corner of her barn. Over in the corner, next to the few bales of hay leftover from the winter, Farmer Fred was putting a very small wire run. He put lots of soft straw and hay in the run, a small bowl of water and another bowl for food. Marigold came over for a closer look. It really was very cosy. It was out of the wind but lit by a ray of sun that came through the old barn door. The small pile of hay provided extra shelter and if Farmer Fred hadn't put that run there, she might have decided to sit there herself.

In a few minutes Farmer Fred came back with a big smart hen under his arm. She was very pretty indeed, with a collar of black feathers on her mostly white plumage, a black tip to her tail and a big red comb. When Marigold looked closely, she could see that the collar feathers were actually black tipped with white, which did look very elegant.

'Hello,' said Marigold. 'I don't think we've met before.'

'Hello,' said the hen in a rather muffled voice because she had a mouth full of hay. The very second Farmer Fred had put her down in the pen, she had started building a nest.

'I am afraid I am a little busy just at this moment, but I will soon have plenty of time to chat.' She bustled around some more, making the nest bigger and warmer.

'Are you planning to lay a lot of eggs then?' asked Marigold politely.

'I have a lot of eggs already,' replied the hen. 'Farmer Fred has just gone to fetch them for me. He'll be back in a minute, so I have a lot to do.' And she turned round and round in her nest.

Just then, back came Farmer Fred with a basket which he was carrying very carefully. It was full of eggs, some white, some brown and some green. These eggs he placed carefully in the nest that the hen had built and then he stood up, stretching his stiff back.

'Well done Millie old girl,' he said to the hen. 'That's a very good nest. Now just you sit on these eggs for me and hatch them out safely.'

Millie, for that was the name of the hen, climbed carefully on top of the eggs, fluffed out her feathers and settled down with a sigh.

'Now I can talk to you Marigold,' she said. 'In fact, I would be glad of a chat whenever you feel like it. I will be sitting here for a good while.'

Marigold thought hard. She didn't want to be rude, but she had a question which she was burning to ask.

'Millie,' she said, taking great care with her question. 'Which are your eggs? The brown ones, the white ones or the funny green ones?'

'They are all mine,' said Millie with a sharp tone in her voice.

‘Oh,’ said Marigold, ‘I didn’t know that hens could lay eggs in different colours.’

‘They are ALL mine,’ repeated Millie and she turned around until she was facing the other way. Marigold took the hint and wandered off.

Days and days went by and still Millie sat on the nest. She took brief breaks to eat, and drink and stretch her legs, but each time she came back she carefully turned all her eggs over and then sat on them again with her black and white feathers all fluffed out. Then one day she got off the nest in great excitement. The eggs were hatching.

First one of the white eggs rolled and twitched and then cracked right open, and a small very pale, yellow chick fell out. Then one of the brown eggs started making a noise. It seemed to have a much tougher shell and it took a long time for the chick to break its way out. When it did it was a dark coloured chick, quite different to the first. Lots more eggs hatched, some with pale chicks and some with dark chicks. Then one of the green eggs hatched. This chick was different again. It was yellow and brown and had a stripy head. By this time the cheeping noise was tremendous, and Marigold felt her brains were going to leak out through her ears. ‘Congratulations Millie,’ she said, and moved away to get some peace.

It was a few days before Marigold saw Millie and her family again. When she did, it was because she heard Millie calling in great distress to her chicks.

‘Come back, oh do come back!’

She had taken all the chicks for a walk in the sunshine. At first all had gone well, and everyone had enjoyed a scratch in the yard. But then they had gone near the pond and suddenly all the chicks with stripy heads had rushed off into the water and paddled away. Millie stood on the bank with all the yellow and dark chicks around her. None of them showed any signs of rushing on to the pond. Millie watched sadly for a while, then heaved a big sigh, settled her feathers again, and took her remaining chicks back to the yard.

'Sorry Millie,' said Farmer Fred who had been watching, 'but ducklings always go home to the pond eventually. You gave them a good start. In fact, the best foster Mum ever!' And he threw some extra corn down for Millie and her genuine hen brood.

More Danger at White Cows

Right in the centre of White Cows Farm, far away from the farmhouse and farm buildings, there is a big copse of trees covering the banks of a small valley. At the bottom of the valley is a little pond, and in the steep banksides there are many badger tunnels. These are the home of the Brock Clan.

The Clan had three families living in the connecting tunnels deep under the earth. The Senior Brocks had a Ma and Pa and two cubs born in February. The Middle Brocks were related to the Seniors, and they too had two new cubs. The New Brocks had arrived in the copse the previous year. After a period of great suspicion and caution, while they got to know all the other resident badgers, they were eventually welcomed and now they lived in the smallest tunnels at the end of the valley. They had just one cub this year but were extra specially proud of their first cub.

On this May evening, there were 5 cubs playing in the valley, chasing each other round the pond and occasionally finding a slug or snail, which they ate with great relish.

The adult badgers were all very busy too. Ma Senior Brock was sitting at the end of the valley, watching the cubs and making sure they played safely. Pa Senior was hunting among the leaf litter, while the other badgers were clearing some old bedding out of tunnels that had had a lot of use during the winter. They all shuffled backwards out of the scruffy tunnels with a big pile of old bedding under their tummies, until they could dump it clear of the tunnel entrance.

Suddenly, Ma Senior Brock sat up straight and made a loud alarm call. The badgers ran for cover, cubs and adults alike. There were three strange men approaching, all carrying spades, ropes and big sacks. The copse was quiet, with not a badger in sight, when the men put down the ropes and sacks and started digging. The badgers underground started to shiver with fright, and to back away down the tunnels to the very deepest level under the tree roots. These wicked men were trying to dig them out! Ma Senior Brock, Ma Middle Brock and Ma New Brock pushed all five cubs behind them at the very end of the deepest tunnel. All the Pa Brocks stood in front, baring their teeth and getting ready to fight. But the men had big sharp spades and the badgers knew who would win in the end.

Soil was beginning to shower down from the roof of the tunnel as the men's spades disturbed the ground, and the badgers were getting very frightened indeed, when Marigold the house cow spotted the strangers and guessed they were up to no good. She looked round for Patch, but she was a long way off, fast asleep in the farmyard. All the golden cows were out in their meadow, so there was no help to be had from them. She was beginning to panic, when Gertie Goose passed by overhead.

'Gertie!' she called. 'Gertie! Quick, we need your help.' Gertie landed with a loud flutter of feathers and waddled over to Marigold.

'What's the problem, Marigold?' she asked.

'Those men, they're after the badgers,' replied Marigold. 'We need you to raise the alarm.'

'Leave it with me,' said Gertie, self-importantly. She turned toward the farmyard, flapped her wings, and with a good run across the field, she succeeded in getting into the air again. Calling loudly, she tilted her wings and as Marigold watched, squinting into the sun, the big white goose glided in a circle and headed for the farmyard.

Wakened from a lovely snooze, Scratchy Patch was a bit grumpy to start with, but soon grasped the danger facing the badgers. She ran to fetch Farmer Fred, and he rang all his neighbours. Very soon, the evil men with the spades found themselves facing 5 angry farmers with shotguns.

'We've rung the police,' said Farmer Fred, 'so get off my land and don't come back'.

The three men hesitated and lifted their spades in a threatening manner. The five farmers lifted their guns and a silence fell that even Patch didn't dare break.

'You won't fire them,' sneered one of the men. 'You won't risk killing someone, so stop pretendin'. Turn around and mind your own business. We'll be gone in an hour, and no harm done.' All three took a step towards the farmers.

'Now there you've made two mistakes,' said Farmer Fred, a lot more calmly than he was feeling. 'One: this is my farm, my land, my badgers, and therefore my business. Two: these guns are loaded with rock salt, not pellets. At least, I think they are. And let me tell you, that while the salt probably won't kill you,' he emphasised *probably* quite a lot, 'it will hurt like the devil. And we will fire, believe me, if you're not off my land by the time I've counted 5. One,' he said, and the farmers took a step towards the men. 'Two!' said Farmer Fred, and the farmers all took another step forwards. Who knows how it would have ended, except at that moment, to Fred's enormous relief, there came the sound of police sirens and the sight of blue flashing lights. The three men broke and ran, but the police were waiting at the end of the lane. The Brock families were safe, and all because of the Farm Watch team of Marigold, Gertie and Patch: and a large box of Mrs Fred's best rock salt.

The Worried Woollies

The largest number of farm animals on White Cows Farm were the animals Patch rudely called the worried woollies. She didn't mean to be rude. She just didn't understand how any animal could smell so strongly of worry ALL THE TIME!

'I mean,' she said to Marigold, one sunny May morning. 'I worried when my puppies got into mischief, and I worry when Farmer Fred goes out that he might not come back. And,' she added thoughtfully, 'I worry just a little bit in the evening that he might forget my supper and I have to look at him like this,' she looked very earnestly at Marigold with big pleading eyes, 'just to remind him.'

'Don't look at me like that,' said Marigold, feeling uncomfortable. 'It makes me feel as though I have to give you something!' And she swished her tail irritably.

'Sorry,' said Patch. 'I was just demonstrating. Anyway, the point is,' she was a very determined dog when she wanted to make her point. 'The point is, I don't worry ALL THE TIME.'

'Perhaps you should go and ask them,' said Marigold and wandered off, grazing. Patch made her way to the meadow near the Broad where the sheep were grazing quietly. At least, the older sheep were grazing. The young ones were still rushing around in a gang, first all down the field, then they'd all turn round and run up the field. Sometimes, the one at the back would still be running down the field when everyone else had turned round and was running up and they'd get bowled over in the rush!

As Patch got near the gate, one of the older ewes on guard duty spotted her and shouted 'Danger. Danger!' And all the ewes collected up their lambs and moved away.

'Now, that's exactly what I mean!' said Patch in frustration. 'I'm not a wolf or a bear, I'm a dog.' And she lay down by the gate trying to look small and unthreatening.

The guard ewe paused and looked over her shoulder. 'All the same to us,' she said shortly.

'But why?' asked Patch. 'Why do you worry and panic all the time?'

The ewe looked at Patch and came a little closer. 'I'll tell you why,' she said. 'You had young uns Patch. What would you do if someone hurt your young uns?'

'Why,' said Patch, all the hair bristling along her neck, 'I'd growl, and I'd bark and I'd bite and I'd really hurt anyone who hurt my pups if they didn't stop!'

'Exactly,' said the ewe, looking rather nervously at Patch who was lifting her lip at the thought. 'Look at me. What would I do?'

'Well, you could bite......' Patch's voice trailed off.

'What with?' asked the ewe. 'My teeth are for grazing grass not biting.'

'Well, Marigold would butt,' said Patch.

'Yes,' said the ewe, 'but Marigold is much bigger, and she has horns. I don't have horns.' Patch thought hard, but she couldn't think of anything.

'All I can do,' said the ewe, 'is get between my lambs and danger, and run away. That's why I worry because there is a lot of danger out there. Crows, magpies, foxes, badgers, nearly all dogs - except you Patch,' she added with some haste. 'Bad men, everything threatens my lambs and me, and all I can do is run away.'

'I'm sorry,' said Patch feeling quite humble. 'I won't call you the worried woollies again.'

'Oh bless you,' said the sheep, laughing heartily, 'we don't mind that. But you could help us. If you spot foreign dogs coming onto the Farm off the lead, like that one the other day, can you run and tell Farmer Fred? They are really, really dangerous!'

I will,' said Patch, 'and I'll get Gertie Goose and Marigold to keep a watch too.'

'Then I'm a lot less worried,' said the old ewe with a twinkle, and went away to feed her two big lambs.

Marigold Gets a Big Surprise

At the very bottom of White Cows Farm the fields slope down to the Ormesby Broad. This is a very special place. At the edge there are willow trees overhanging the water, and a big thicket of elder, alder and brambles. One sunny June day, Marigold and Patch had gone there for a quiet graze (for Marigold) and a little hunt through the brambles (for Patch). Marigold had done her grazing and Patch had done her hunting, although she'd had only a sniff of a rabbit. Now they were both tired and hot. They found a good area of shade under a big willow and they both sat down, Marigold to chew the cud and Patch to pant and scratch.

They hadn't been sitting there for long when Marigold said, 'I'm thirsty Patch. I'm just popping down to the water for a drink.' She heaved herself to her feet and wandered quietly down to the Broad. Patch thumped the ground with her tail once, twice, but stayed where she was, cooling down under the tree. Marigold put her head down to the water and started to suck it in. She was quite a noisy sucker, making a noise like someone being rude with a straw. Just as she was finishing her drink, she got a big surprise. A head popped up out of the water, right under her nose. The head was furry and brown and quite flat. It had big dark eyes and small rounded ears set low. The head was attached to a long body with short legs but a very big strong tail. Marigold picked her head up very suddenly, dribbling water everywhere, and made a surprised noise.

'Mu!'

'Sssh,' said the otter, for an otter it was. 'There's a dog over there. Don't wake it up! Hello cow, I am Ottalie the otter and I've just moved in.'

'Hello Ottalie,' boomed Marigold, 'welcome!'

'Sssh,' said Ottalie again, 'you'll wake the dog!'

'Oh Patch is alright,' said Marigold a bit more quietly, 'she's a friend of mine.'

'She might be a very good friend to you, but she'll chase me and my cubs,' said the Otter. 'Dogs just do.'

Marigold thought of all the things that Patch did chase - the rabbits, the squirrels, the seagulls, the pigeons - she had to admit the list was a long one.

'Ok,' she said, mooing very quietly now. Or at least, quietly for a large cow. 'I know what you mean. I'll keep quiet. Are you going to live here now!'

'Yes,' said Ottalie. 'I have my holt under the tree roots in there.' And she nodded in the direction of the thicket of elder and alder.

'This is a good place,' she added, 'lots of fish and a good slope to build a slide on.'

'Where were you before?' asked Marigold, settling down for a long chat.

'I lived with my cubs on the River Ant,' she replied. That was a good place too. Lots of eels. I like eels. Especially the little ones. Did you know you can see right through them? Like glass?'

No, I didn't know that,' answered Marigold. 'Why did you move here?'

For a moment the otter looked sad. She splashed some water over her nose with her paws, sneezed, then looked up. 'It's not a happy story,' she said.

'Not dog related?' asked Marigold, looking up the hill to where Patch was snoozing happily in the shade, her paws twitching as she chased something in her dreams.

'No. It wasn't a dog. It was a fisherman.'

Marigold looked up, surprised. 'I didn't know fishermen were a problem to anything except fish,' she said, her brain filled with pictures of fishermen diving into rivers after otters, or sliding down muddy slopes with their arms waving in the air.

'That's the problem,' said Ottalie. 'They fish! That's bad enough. They take fish that we could eat, and sometimes they don't even eat them! How stupid is that? But worst of all, they don't care what happens to their gear after they stop fishing.'

Marigold thought about how she felt when Farmer Fred mowed his lawn and threw all the grass in a pile. Grass she could have eaten! She felt quite cross for a moment. Then she reminded herself that it didn't happen very often. Farmer Fred would never mow the lawn at all, if Mrs Fred didn't threaten him with *'NO CAKE'* if he didn't do something about what she called the hayfield in their garden.

'Sorry, I don't understand. What do they do?' she mooed.

Ottalie pulled herself a little further onto the bank. 'This one, the fisherman that caused all the trouble, he got his line caught on a rock in the river, and when he couldn't pull it clear, he cut it off and left it in the water.' Marigold had a horrible feeling she could see where this story was going.

'What happened then?' she asked.

'My cubs were playing in the river one day, chasing each other round and round the rock. One of them got caught in the fishing line. The others came to fetch me, and I rushed over. The river was flowing very fast. I could only just see the line. It was almost clear, like a baby eel, but so dangerous. I tried very hard to chew through the line, I was so afraid. And I did manage to free my cub from the rock.'

'Well, that was good, wasn't it?' asked Marigold, quietly uncrossing her front hooves.

Ottalie wiped a tear from her eye. 'Yes, at least she didn't drown,' she said. 'But the trouble wasn't over. I couldn't get the line from round her neck, and as she grew, it cut into her flesh. She was very brave, but it was so painful.'

'What happened next?' whispered Marigold, hardly daring to ask.

'Eventually, it hurt so much she couldn't swim any more, and one day when she was lying on the bank, some people wearing bright tabards saying 'rescue' came and carried her away on a stretcher.'

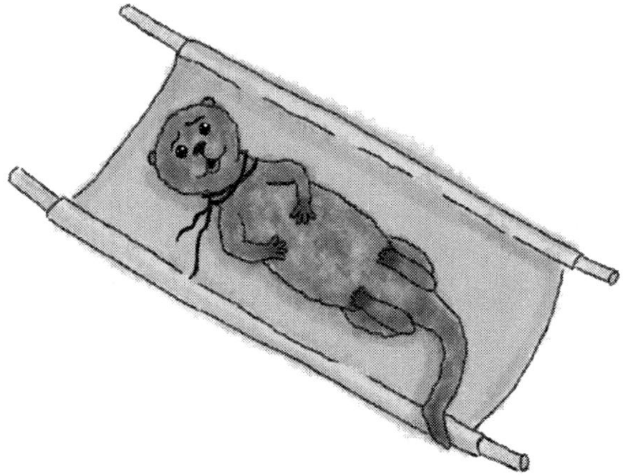

Much relieved, Marigold started to cud again. She'd been so worried by the sad story, she'd had to stop. 'Well, that's *good* news,' she said. 'They'll have taken her away and made her better.'

'But I couldn't stay in such a dangerous place. That's why I came here. For the sake of the other cubs. But now I'll never seen her again, even if they do make her better,' wailed Ottalie.

Marigold leaned out over the lake and tried to look comforting. 'But at least you know she was looked after' she said. 'And here you can raise your other cubs in safety.' She stuck her tongue up each nostril in turn, as cows will, and Ottalie recoiled a little.

'Yes, that's true,' she said. 'Whoops!' That dog is waking up!'

With scarcely a splash she slid down in the water and started to swim away.

'Bring your cubs to see me next time,' cried Marigold as Ottalie disappeared, then she looked round as Patch arrived, sniffing very suspiciously.

'Who've you been talking to Marigold?' she asked, still sniffing. 'I can tell something was here. Not a rat surely! Smells a bit fishy for a rat!'

'It was a very nice new resident named Ottalie,' said Marigold severely, 'and if you promise not to chase her, I might introduce you next time!'

'Uff,' said Patch, and sat down for another scratch.

Late July

In late July, the weather turned unusually warm at White Cows Farm. The geese and ducks spent a lot of time on the farm pond, although Gertie was very worried that it might shrink to nothing.

'Just look at this,' she said to Marigold, slapping her big, broad foot on the expanse of dry mud around the edges of the pond.

'It has dried up a lot,' agreed Marigold. 'Don't worry Gertie. It's happened before and it will happen again. It'll refill when it rains.' She stepped forward onto the mud and put her head down to take a drink.

'Don't do that,' shrieked Gertie, flapping her wings at Marigold, who reared back in surprise.

'What's the problem?' asked Marigold, looking round to see what danger was approaching now.

'There's little enough water for us to swim on as it is. Don't you make things worse by drinking it!' The level of disgust in Gertie's voice had to be heard to be believed.

'Well very sorry I'm sure,' said Marigold, very offended. And she marched off into the barn to drink from a water trough. 'It's too hot to be out there in the sun anyway,' she muttered, as she dribbled all over the barn floor.

Indeed, every animal on the farm was staying out of the sun. Marigold sheltered in the barn, the sheep lay under the trees, and moved around during the day as the patch of shade moved with the sun. The pigs made lovely soggy wallows and lay in them, making sure they were well covered with mud. Even the bees seemed to be flying slower than usual. Patch, the spaniel, alternated between the cool flagstones of the hall floor and the barn, where a particular spot near the door caught what little breeze there was.

This particular day, she was still lying at the entrance to the barn as the sun went down. Marigold, pottering off for her evening graze, found her shaking her head, and scratching at her ears.

'What's the matter Patch?' she asked. 'Fleas again?'

'No,' snapped Patch, rather grumpily. 'And don't be so rude. I've only had fleas once and it wasn't my fault. I got them off Needles, the hedgehog.'

'You should leave her alone, then you wouldn't be close enough to catch her fleas,' counselled Marigold.

'I only rolled her about a bit with my paw,' objected Patch. 'Anyway, I haven't got fleas. But I have got an annoying noise in my ears. I think there must be something wrong with them.'

'What sort of noise?' asked Marigold. 'I can't hear anything.'

'That's my point,' said Patch. 'It's a sort of high-pitched peeping. But it seems no-one else can hear it. Are you sure you can't hear it? It's maddening.' She shook her head again, making her big ears flap about like wings. Marigold looked up at the sky, and started to laugh.

'Now what?' asked Patch, pausing her ear flapping. 'What's so funny?'

'You,' said Marigold. 'Look up Patch, and I think you'll see where your problems are coming from.'

Patch looked up. The sky was dark by the trees, but there was a lighter patch between the branches and the barn roof. As she watched, she saw tiny shapes zigging and zagging in the sky. When one of the zig zags flew immediately over her head, she heard a particularly loud squeak at the same time.

'Oh!' she exclaimed. 'It's them. What are they?'

'It's the bats,' said Marigold. 'Haven't you ever seen them before?'

'I don't think I have,' replied Patch. Her face was turned to the sky, and as she followed the flight of the closest bat over her head, she leaned back so far she nearly fell over. 'I'm normally in the house at this time of the evening. And I've never seen them when I come out for my last walk around.'

'They only fly around at this time,' said Marigold. 'I've seen them often, but I can't talk to them because I can't hear them. Their voices are too high.'

'I wish I couldn't hear them,' complained Patch. 'They talk even more than Gertie. They talk all the time!'

'That's not talking,' said Marigold. 'It's how they find their way around in the dark. They make a squeak, then when it bounces off an object the echo tells them where they are. At least, that's what I heard Farmer Fred say to his granddaughter, little Liesl.'

'Well I wish they wouldn't bounce them off my head,' muttered Patch.

She sat in the moonlight by the barn door, and watched some more. There were lots of the little shapes darting about above her head.

'What are they doing?' she asked Marigold, and was very surprised when one of the little shapes came to a sudden stop on the barn door.

'Catching supper,' it squeaked in a very high, tiny voice.

Patch looked at it solemnly for a moment. It was only the size of a small plum, with funny, fabric wings attached to what, in anything else, would be its legs.

'You do realise you're hanging upside down,' she remarked. 'All the blood will run to your head.'

The bat made another tiny squeaking noise which Patch took to be laughter. 'Upside down is right side up for us,' it replied.

While Patch tried to work that out, Marigold joined in.

'What's it saying?', she asked. 'I can't hear anything.'

'It says it's hunting its supper,' said Patch. 'What do you eat?' she asked the bat.

'Insects,' said the bat. 'And I need to catch some more. I've only had two thousand, four hundred and thirty-two so far tonight.' And without a moments delay, it flew off and rejoined the zigging and zagging in the sky above them.

Patch explained to Marigold what the bat had said.

'Two thousand, four hundred and how many?' asked Marigold. 'You must have misheard.'

'Patch opened her mouth to say, *'no she hadn't,'* when the bat flew past again.

'Two thousand, eight hundred now,' it squeaked. 'Wheee. Nearly there. Two hundred more and I can call it a day.'

The Great Escape

When Patch had all her puppies with her on the farm, they once had an exciting tour around the farm, taking in the worried woollies, Gertie Goose, and a very large animal named Sally the Sow. She had lots of piglets which were very interested in the puppies until their food arrived, then they lost all interest in a way that the puppies had thought very rude. Very rude indeed!

The piglets weren't so small now. While the puppies had grown up and gone to their forever homes, the piglets had got bigger too. Some of the lady piglets had already been sold. They were special pedigree pigs and they had gone to new homes where they too would have piglets of their own. They were called Saddlebacks, because they had a black mark on their backs that looked like a saddle.

There were two boy piglets left and they were getting quite big and cheeky. Farmer Fred had decided they should move to a new sty all of their own, and asked Patch if she would help. Patch didn't think this was a very good idea. She was not a sheepdog and not used to herding things. She was definitely not used to herding something much bigger than she was. And ESPECIALLY she was not used to herding something with teeth bigger than hers!

It didn't go very well.

Farmer Fred opened the door to the old sty and encouraged the two boys, Pepe and Pablo, out into the farmyard. They didn't take much encouraging. With a grunt and a squeak, they were off. They stuck their little curly tails in the air, and they galloped straight for Patch.

'Stop them Patch,' roared Farmer Fred.

'You stop them,' muttered Patch, as two very fat, very energetic, very over-excited pigs ran straight at her. Both her ears and her tail went down, and she slunk to one side. Then she barked a lot.

'Row row row row,' she said. But that was mainly to hide her embarrassment.

'Oh Patch,' said Farmer Fred, and he ran off down the yard in his old wellies, puffing and blowing. By the time he got to the far gate, Pepe and Pablo had vanished.

Patch could have told him where they had gone. Her nose told her exactly the route they had taken, but by then she was in a serious sulk and had gone back to her nest in the barn. Pablo and Pepe had gone out of the gate, down the field, and were hiding in the old trees by the Broad. They had everything they wanted there: lots of soft earth to dig in for roots, worms and insects, lots of trees to browse, lots of old dead leaves to make a nest in, water nearby, and even a big field to wander in. They only thing they missed was the food delivered to them twice daily, but the little wood was so much more exciting than their old pen.

It took Farmer Fred a couple of hours to find them. He looked at the wood, and the big field, and the contented porkers. Then he scratched his head and had a think.

Next day, he hitched up his battered trailer to his old tractor. Then, he loaded into the trailer a pig ark, a feed trough, a big bale of straw and a bag of pig nuts. At the last minute, Patch jumped into the trailer, just so she could see what was going on. The old tractor and the tatty trailer bumped and jolted down the field all the way to the wood by the Broad. When they got there, Patch jumped off and went to have a sniff around. It was obvious to her that Pablo and Pepe were still in the trees. Farmer Fred unloaded the pig ark. It hit the hard ground behind the trailer with a bang and a rattle but stayed in one piece. Then he put the straw inside the ark, unloaded the feed trough with another loud clang and tipped the pig nuts into it. They rattled loudly as they hit the metal. Pablo and Pepe emerged from the trees, sniffing, and looking around suspiciously.

'It's alright lads,' said Farmer Fred. 'This big dog won't hurt you.' Patch glared at him. 'No call to be sarcastic,' she muttered.

'Here you are boys,' went on Farmer Fred. 'If this is where you want to live, that's ok with me. I've brought you some shelter for when the weather is bad, and I'll feed you just like before. How's that?'

Pablo and Pepe looked pleased and might have said thank you, but they had their mouths full of pignuts.

Patch and the Geese

One early morning, Patch, found herself sharing the farmyard with a whole gaggle of geese. There was Gertie, the acknowledged boss of the yard. (Acknowledged by Gertie anyway. Marigold the house cow wouldn't have agreed, but she wouldn't have picked a fight with Gertie either). As well as Gertie, there was Gerald, her husband, and a whole lot of goslings. Patch knew Gladys, Graham, Gail, Gary, Gilbert, Gulliver, Grace, Gabrielle and Guinevere, but there were some others whose names she didn't know.

When she said this, Gertie offered to introduce her, but as Patch said, if she had to remember any more names beginning with g, she would have to go away and gargle!

'What are you going to do when you run out of g names Gertie?' she asked.

'Start again at the beginning!' said Gertie, as if talking to a nincompoop. Patch felt a little indignant but knew there was no point arguing with Gertie. She was always right. And when she wasn't right everyone else was wrong! You couldn't win an argument with Gertie.

Gertie and Gerald sidled up to each other and pecked a bit at each other's beaks. Patch knew that Gertie and Gerald had been together forever, raising goslings and protecting the farmyard from invaders. Gerald was very fierce with invaders, in which category he included just about everybody except Farmer Fred and Mrs Fred, but he was putty in Gertie's beak, and everyone knew it.

The billing and cooing, or at least the billing over with, Gertie turned to Patch and said, 'It's story time for goslings. Would you like to join us Patch?'

'Well that depends,' said Patch, with some hard-earned caution, 'on whether I have heard it before. Is it going to be the one about how geese saved Ancient Rome from the invading Gauls, or the one about the goose that laid the golden egg?'

'Neither,' said Gertie huffily, 'I thought we might have the one about the goddess whose chariot was drawn by geese...'

'Heard it,' said Patch.

'.... or the one about Mother Goose?

'Heard that too,' said Patch.

'OR,' said Gertie raising her voice quite a lot, 'the one about the Iceland Grey Goose laws?'

'I think you're making that up,' exclaimed Patch, and anyway, don't you know any non-Goose-related stories?'

'I am not making it up,' said Gertie, her bill getting hot with rage. 'The laws were written with Goose quills and bound in Goose skin. And I would like to see anyone writing laws with Spaniel feathers!' And she marched off, very cross, with her big feet making a slapping noise on the ground and her tail waggling from side to side. All the goslings followed her, with Gerald bringing up the rear.

'Today,' said Gertie loudly as they settled down by the pond, 'we will have the story about how the very silly spaniel chased a wild goose and failed to catch it, and how this is where the saying a "wild goose chase" came from.'

'She's definitely making that up,' muttered Patch sulkily, but Gerald was still in earshot.

'Apologise tomorrow,' he hissed to Patch, 'when she's calmed down, and all will be well.'

Melissas

It was a sunny day and Marigold was sitting thinking. She spent a lot of time doing that. After all, a cow has to do something during all those hours of chewing the cud. So today she was sitting and thinking about flying things. Not just any flying things. The small ones with lots of legs.

She manoeuvred another cud into her mouth and readjusted her forelegs into a more comfortable position as she started chewing again.

'Small flying things,' she mused, 'can be divided into two sorts. The ones that are really, really annoying and need to be swatted by my tail (and she waved her tail about to demonstrate what she meant) 'and the other sort that leave me alone. And,' she thought further, concentrating very hard, 'that second sort are also two sorts. The very pretty ones that flutter about playing games all day; and the chunky sort that buzz and look very busy all the time.'

As Marigold was lying near a field of flowering oilseed rape, there were lots of the buzzing sort around her at the time. Some were flying towards the flowers, some were busy in the flowers, and some were flying away from the flowers. When she looked closely, the ones flying away looked heavy and were carrying bags of yellow stuff, so when she'd finished cudding, she decided to see where they were going.

It wasn't far. They were all flying to and from the white boxes that Farmer Fred's friend Jo had put near the field a week or two ago. Very cautiously, just in case they suddenly turned into the other sort of flyers and started to bother her, she crept towards the boxes to see what they were doing. As she got closer, a guard bee (for bees they were) stopped her with a loud buzz. It had such a tiny voice Marigold wasn't sure at first it was talking to her, but it was telling her not to come closer in case she stepped on their hive.

'And stop waving your tail around please,' buzzed the bee politely, 'you might hit my sister.'

'Oh sorry,' said Marigold. 'Which is your sister?'

'All of them,' said the bee, perching on a daisy and checking it over for pollen. It didn't have much though, so close to the hive.

'What! All of them!' exclaimed Marigold. 'How do you remember all their names? She was thinking of Gerties' much smaller brood of goslings with their many names all beginning with g.

'That's easy,' said the bee, cleaning her antennae with her legs. 'We are all named Melissa, which means "bee".'

While Marigold was thinking hard about that, the bee said 'Whoops, I need to be off. My turn on collecting duty.' And she buzzed into the air.

'Hang on,' said Marigold, 'collecting what?' But the first Melissa had already gone.

'Nectar and pollen from the flowers,' said a second Melissa, taking over the bees' side of the conversation, 'for us and our grubs to eat.'

'I like flowers too,' said Marigold, trying to find common ground with the bees, 'but I only get them sort of by accident when I am eating grass. Except buttercups,' she added with a shudder. 'I don't like those at all. They are bitter.'

'We don't like those either,' said Melissa 2. 'They are poisonous and can kill us.'

'What flowers do you like?' asked Marigold with interest.

'Well,' said Melissa 3, taking over from the second bee who had flown off, 'we like the yellow rape-flowers and there are lots of those now, and we like all the fruit tree blossoms, and we especially like garden flowers like lavender. We are told,' said Melissa 4 dreamily, 'that in the north of this county there are whole fields of lavender. Acres and acres. That would be heaven.'

Marigold wandered off to graze, being very careful what she did with her tail, and thinking of hundreds of Melissas, all dreaming of a heaven full of lavender fields.

Rory

Reading about Marigold, you may have wondered why she had so much time to just sit around, thinking and chatting to passing bees. Well, the answer, of course, is that she is on her annual holiday. Cows can only give milk if they have a calf, and as Marigold's creamy milk is very important to Farmer Fred and Mrs Fred, she is currently awaiting the arrival of her latest calf.

'And,' as Mrs Fred said bitterly, on her way to buy supermarket milk, 'that means no milk from Marigold for a short while.'

So Marigold is on holiday, with no work to do except graze, chew the cud, chat with Patch and anyone else who has the time to spare, and basically just hang about watching her sides get wider and wider as her calf grows.

In short, Marigold is bored. She has talked to Patch, the pigs, the sheep, Gertie and Gerald, and the bees. She tried the goslings, but they were young and silly, and just gobbled at her. She tried Eostre the hare, but she was moving too fast. In fact, everyone seems to move away now, when they see her coming. Which is how Marigold came to be pottering about in the edge of the wood near the Broad.

She shouldn't really have been there at all. Strictly speaking she was the wrong side of the fence, and the fence had a distinctly Marigold-shaped hole in it. But, with nothing better to do, she decided to go for an explore.

Still full of grass from the meadow, she nonetheless had space to try some fresh new leaves off the trees, and even a bit of bark, when her happy browsing was interrupted. Right in front of her was a small brown fawn with a few pale spots, curled up in the grass. He was so still, and so well hidden, she nearly stepped on him.

'Whoa,' she exclaimed. 'What are you doing there all on your own?' The fawn said nothing and didn't even look at her.

'I say,' she said, trying again, 'are you lost?' Still nothing. If anything, the fawn curled up tighter.

'Or deaf and lost?' asked Marigold, putting her nose down to sniff him. As she did so, she licked her nose, putting her tongue neatly up each nostril, and dribbled slightly on the fawn.

'Ugh,' he exclaimed. 'Don't do that. My mummy told me not to talk to strangers!'

'Sorry I'm sure,' said Marigold, a little offended. 'But I just wanted to be sure you were alright.'

'I'm fine,' said the fawn, putting his head back in the hollow of grass. 'Mummy hasn't been gone long. When the sun reaches the top of that tree,' and he pointed with his nose, 'she'll be back, and I'll get my lunch.'

'Oh,' said Marigold. 'Does she leave you all day?'

'Oh yes,' replied the fawn, 'until I'm bigger. Then I'll go with her. But for now, I stay in our safe place, and she comes back with my meals. But she won't come if there's a crowd,' he added pointedly, and put his head down again.

Marigold took the hint and returned to the (slightly broken) fence. But just as she reached the edge of the wood, she looked back. There in the tree shadows was an elegant shape, slipping silently through the brambles to the place where the fawn lay. As she watched, the fawn got up and started to suckle, while his mother sniffed suspiciously at the spot on his back where Marigold had dribbled.

'Sorry!' whispered Marigold and went back to the meadows where she belonged.

MARIGOLD'S BIG DAY

Mrs Fred was surprised to see Marigold hanging around the farmyard. While on her holiday Marigold had a free run of most of the farm. Even, as Mrs Fred wryly noted, some bits she wasn't supposed to be in. (Her foray into the wood last month had not gone unnoticed. Nor had the Marigold-shaped hole in the fence but, as Mrs Fred said to Farmer Fred when he complained about having to fill in the hole, he might mutter about her little ways but he was first in line for clotted cream with his scones when she was milking.)

Anyway, what she didn't usually do was hang about in the barn once she had begged her morning treat from the back door (usually an apple or some carrots). Mrs Fred watched a little then called 'Fred! Fred, I think Marigold must be due!'

'Due what?' asked Fred who wasn't at his best in the morning until he had had his second breakfast - the big one with eggs and bacon after he had finished the morning chores.

'Due to have her calf!' exclaimed Mrs F with exasperation. 'What have we been waiting for all this time?'

Fred went to have a look at Marigold, who looked back at him. She wasn't giving anything away. Ok, she might have felt inclined to stay near the house, just in case help was needed, but she wasn't going to say so.

This went on all day. Every now and then, Farmer Fred and Marigold would exchange long looks. In between times Mrs F came out with little treats, which Marigold accepted politely. Patch came to have a look too, but even to her Marigold wasn't saying anything.

'So,' said Patch, sitting down and scratching an ear with a handy hind leg with a thoroughness that explained her full name (Scratchy Patch). 'Calf due then?'

Marigold sniffed and stuck her tongue up her nose.

'In due course,' she said, which was something she had heard Mrs F say to the grandchildren when they asked what time supper would be. She didn't know precisely what it meant, but it seemed a useful phrase. Patch scratched the other ear.

'When's that?' she asked. There was never any messing about with Patch. Marigold sighed and retreated further into the barn. Truth was, she knew something was about to happen, but she didn't know precisely when. But she was sure nothing was going to happen with everyone looking at her.

Supper time came and went, and nothing changed. Bedtime came and Farmer Fred had a last look round to make sure everything and Marigold was alright. Marigold gave him another of her long looks and sighed heavily. By midnight, everything was quiet, and Marigold began to think she might get some peace.

But at 2 o'clock on the stable clock, blow me if Farmer Fred didn't reappear in his jimjams, poking and prying again.

'I don't believe it,' exploded Marigold. 'What does a cow have to do round here to get a bit of privacy?' And she stomped off into the corner of the barn. It was a quiet corner, out of the wind, nice pile of straw and even some hay. In fact, it was very close to where Patch had her puppies, and where the hen reared her chicks.

'Aha,' said Fred to himself quietly, and went back to the farmhouse kitchen. But he didn't go back to bed. Instead, he pulled a kitchen chair close to the Aga, opened the oven door for extra warmth, and sat down with the paper. After an hour or so, he went back to the barn, but he didn't go in. Instead, he peered through a hole in the timbers.

'Aha,' he said again, and went back to his paper.

In the very early morning Farmer Fred made one last trip to the barn.

'Well done Marigold old girl,' he said. 'Well done.' And he squirted antibiotic on the new calf's navel and checked her over. Marigold looked very happy with her calf, and very smug too because she had managed it all on her own. She didn't know, of course, that Farmer Fred had kept an eye on her all night, and Patch wasn't saying anything either.

After first breakfast (cereal) Mrs F came quietly in to admire the new calf too.

'My turn to name her,' she said. 'You named the last one Fred. And we did agree we would keep this one.'

'Yes, I did, so pick a good name,' he answered. And they all waited while Mrs F thought hard.

'Well,' said Mrs F, 'it needs to be another flower name, and a pretty one because she is so beautiful, with her golden coat and blue nose. I know, how about Bluebell? It sort of fits too, with Marigold's visit to the wood last month where the bluebells grow when they're in season.'

So Bluebell it was, and while everyone else went into the house for second breakfast, Bluebell got her first ever breakfast from her mother.

Marigold and Bluebell

Bluebell is Hard Work

You will remember that last month Marigold had her long-awaited calf and Mrs Fred named her Bluebell. Since then, Bluebell has done lots of growing, and after morning milking and morning feeding, she and Marigold are turned out into the pastures to graze. This is Bluebell's chance to top up her breakfast bucket of milk (provided by Mrs Fred) with any that Marigold might have left after she is milked. There's never very much, but that way everyone gets a bit of a share of Marigold's special rich milk.

Marigold, however, is discovering that it is no easy ride being the on-duty mother of an energetic calf. No sooner has she filled up with new grass and sat down for a good old cud, than Bluebell is getting into mischief (or trouble - not much difference really thought Marigold) and her poor old mum is having to heave herself to her feet and go and sort out the mess.

First it was the piglets. Ok, yes, they do make a lot of squeaking noises, and they are very inquisitive, and they do look exactly like mobile sausages, but was that a good reason for Bluebell to fall into their wallow? Farmer Fred had to pull her out covered in black mud and he got very muddy himself in the process. Patch thought it was very funny and got the giggles which left her with hiccups, but Farmer Fred was not very amused.

Then Bluebell got in a battle with Gertie Goose. She hadn't meant to be rude when she sat by the pond right where Gertie wanted to sit, and that had ended peaceably in the end when Bluebell offered herself as a perch for the goslings. It was just a pity she ended up wearing two of them like a big, animated hat for the rest of the day.

Yesterday had been a day of poking her nose where it was not wanted. First, she had stuck it on a nettle, and Bluebell's nose was not yet nettle proof. Then she stuck it on Needles, the hedgehog. Needles was of course curled up at the time, so that was another bad experience for a nose that was already traumatised by nettles. Needles wasn't too pleased either. She uncurled just enough to show Marigold an eye and snorted loudly. It was a very expressive snort.

Today had been going well, but at lunchtime it all went horribly downhill. There was Marigold, minding her own business as usual and there was Bluebell, playing games with Boris, the other calf born that month. The calves were having a great game, round the paddock and in and out of the trees, when suddenly where there had been two calves there was only one. Boris came dashing over to his Mum, bellowing his head off, and there was no sign of Bluebell.

Marigold cantered over, calling for her calf, and stopped dead on the edge of the ditch. Somehow, in their game, Boris and Bluebell had broken the hedge by the ditch and Bluebell had fallen in. This was a very different thing to the wallow. The ditch had water in and had very steep sides. Bluebell was trapped with only her head above the water and couldn't get out. She kept trying, but got nowhere, and the effort was tiring her out. Marigold rushed up and down the bank, torn between wanting to stay with her calf and wanting to fetch help. Luckily, at that moment Patch came over to see what joke Bluebell had created this time. She took in the situation at a glance and dashed off to fetch Farmer Fred.

Fred had learned from long experience that when Patch barked that particular bark, he needed to see what the problem was. His heart sank when he saw Bluebell's predicament. This was not a problem he could solve on his own. He whipped out his phone and dialled 999 for the fire brigade.

Later, when Bluebell was safe and warm again, and Patch had a specially nice tea (and a drink of Marigold's milk) to say thank you, Marigold remembered how very kind the fire brigade had been, and how very gently they had lifted Bluebell from the ditch with a giant balloon and ropes.

'Bluebell,' she sighed, 'please can you stay out of trouble tomorrow? We all need a rest.'

OWLS

It was evening at White Cows Farm. In October the evenings were drawing in and from her post at the entrance to the old barn, Marigold could see the last of the swallows wheeling and swooping in the darkening sky. She knew that if she waited just a little longer, she would see the smaller shapes of the bats with their swift and jerky flights as they chased the autumn moths. As she stood, reflectively chewing and viewing, she was startled by a high-pitched screech and then doubly startled by the silent swoop of a large white bird, as it narrowly missed her horns on its way into the barn.

'I do wish you wouldn't do that,' she said irritably to the large Barn Owl perched on the barn partition. The Owl settled her feathers, preening each one into place. 'Couldn't you be a bit noisier? All that silent flying really gets on my horns, especially when you do it just *past* my horns?'

'I can't fly noisily,' said the Owl. 'My feathers are specially designed for stealth flying. And if your head will take up all the space in the barn doorway, how else can I get past? I did let you have a warning hoot!'

'And that's another thing,' said Marigold, not at all appeased. 'Why can't you hoot properly? With a decent tu whit tu whoo? Then I'd know to duck. All you do is screech!'

'That is a proper barn owl call,' said the Owl with dignity. 'No Owl in the world makes a tu whit tu whoo!'

'Oh yes they do,' contradicted Marigold. 'I've heard them in the wood.'

'No they don't,' said the Owl. 'Those are my cousins, the tawny owls, and take it from me, they don't go tu whit tu whoo. What you have been listening to is their duet. My cousin Fi Tawny calls kee-whick, and her mate Bo Tawny answers Whoo whoo. I blame that chap Shakespeare.' she added. 'It was him that described Owl calls as tu whit tu whoo and everyone has got it wrong since.'

'Oh,' said Marigold, 'I didn't know that. How very interesting! Could I meet Fi and Bo?'

'Well,' said the Barn Owl, 'you would have to be out in the fields by the wood at night. That would be the best chance of seeing them. They hunt the fields at night and live in the wood. Look out for an owl a bit smaller than me and a lot browner. I'll tell them you're friendly.

Now, I'm off out again. Duck!'

And the Barn Owl sailed silently into the night sky.

The Arrival of the Fat Pony

Marigold the House Cow was very interested, very interested indeed.

'Hey Patch,' she called, 'we've got a new arrival!'

Patch came scurrying round the corner of the barn, but just at that moment, Gertie Goose and all her family set up a tremendous calling and honking, and the whole lot of them started waddling round and round a small trailer in the yard, towed behind a scruffy Land Rover.

Farmer Fred came out from the house, pulling his braces up over his shoulders. Clearly he had just been disturbed in the middle of his afternoon nap.

'Come on Missus,' he called, 'the pony has arrived.'

The driver of the Land Rover was still behind the wheel. Every time he tried to get out, Gertie beaked him viciously, and he had to slam the door shut again. He wound the window down.

'Hi Fred,' he shouted. 'Come and convince this guard goose of yours that I'm delivering, not stealing.'

'Back to your pond Gertie old girl,' said Farmer Fred, as he shooed Gertie and her brood away behind the gate and closed it. Gertie waddled off, her tail wagging from side to side, clearly very pleased with herself.

'I bet that will be added to Gertie's tales of how geese save the day,' remarked Marigold. 'Now we need to see what's arrived.'

'Fred said it was a pony,' remarked Patch, and at just that moment the stranger was letting down the ramp at the back of the trailer and leading out a small, hairy pony. Mrs Fred seemed very excited and made a big fuss of the newcomer, while the stranger said to Farmer Fred, 'it's very good of you to foster her Fred, I'm sure she'll be very happy here.'

'No trouble at all,' said Fred. 'It's sad her old family can't keep her, and we have plenty of space. But I'm afraid we haven't another horse for her to share a paddock with, so if she gets lonely we may have to think again. She can go in with Marigold for the moment and we'll see how they get on.'

'See,' hissed Marigold to Patch, 'it's coming to live with me. I hope it's a nice pony.'

'It's very hairy,' said Patch critically, 'but it's hard to see how nice it is while Mrs Fred is all over it.'

After a while, Mrs Fred seemed to get over her excitement and she led the pony over to the small paddock where Marigold was leaning over the gate.

'Back off a bit Marigold,' she panted as she struggled with the big old gate. 'I need to put this little lass in with you.' She led the pony through the gate and closed it. 'Let's see how you get on,' she said, 'play nicely now.'

'Play,' huffed Marigold, 'PLAY! What does she think I am? A dog?' Patch smirked, but Marigold politely sniffed at the new arrival, nonetheless.

'I'm Marigold the house cow,' she said. 'Who are you?'

The pony looked up from where she was grazing. 'My proper name is Jumping Jezebel,' she said through a mouthful of grass, 'but you can call me Fat Pony. Everyone else does.' She went back to the grass.

'That seems a bit rude,' said Marigold.

'Not really,' said Fat Pony. 'I am only a little plump, but they call me that because I never stop eating. I don't mind. It's meant to be friendly.' She went back to the grass.

'You are quite wide for your height,' said Marigold assessingly. She looked at Fat Pony, but all she could see was a swishy tail and a round rump. The pony was eating again.

'That's the way I'm made,' said Fat Pony indistinctly, through a big mouthful of grass. 'I'm a Shetland pony. That's just how we are. Short, round and greedy.' She munched on, across the paddock. Marigold could see that, given the progress she had made so far, it wouldn't be very long before she had eaten everything. She needed to get eating herself before it all went into Fat Pony. She put her head down and started grazing.

'There,' said Mrs Fred fondly, 'isn't that nice. Friends already.' Patch hid a smile.

When Marigold had filled herself up, she settled down to cud.

'Hey, Fat Pony,' she called, 'why don't you come and cud with me and we can get to know each other a bit.'

'I don't cud,' said Fat Pony, 'but I can chat for a little while. What do you want to know?'

'Well,' said Marigold, 'how did you come to be here for a start. Oh, and meet Patch. She's a good dog and only chases the things she should. Well, mainly,' she added, just to be completely truthful. Patch joined them in the shade under the apple tree.

Fat Pony found a conveniently low bough to scratch on and replied, 'my last owner grew out of me. She got too big and too heavy and had to get a bigger pony. It's happened before,' she said sadly, 'several times before. I'm only big enough for children you see, and they all grow up.' She scratched again, and then picked up another mouthful of grass.

Marigold and Patch looked at each other.

'That's very sad,' said Marigold, and Patch interrupted, 'but it won't happen here. Mrs Fred is really, really pleased to have you, and I heard her say that, if you are happy, this will be your forever home. There are no children here to grow away from you. Here you can just enjoy the farm and us.'

'And the grass,' said Fat Pony and took another enormous mouthful.

'Yes, about the grass...' said Marigold.

Three Sorts of Goats

The first indication of something new was Farmer Fred banging and clattering in the paddock next to Marigold's. She and Fat Pony trotted up to the fence to watch. First, he went rushing round the field, mending all the dodgy bits of fencing that Marigold had had her eye on as potential escape routes, had she the mind. Fat Pony had wondered about escape too, but as Marigold had unkindly pointed out, she'd need to go on a diet first to get through any of the holes. They'd all gone now anyway; mended, reinforced and even, in some places, raised higher too.

'Now what's he getting,' wondered Marigold aloud. 'A three-day-event horse?' Fat Pony snorted.

'Not on that grass,' she said. 'Nowhere near smart enough. Look, it's all full of baby trees and weeds.'

It wasn't a very smart field, that was true. It was an odd, triangular corner that had been leftover when the farm had been re-fenced many years ago and had never been used for much. Occasionally Marigold had a bit of a browse. Sometimes the geese went in to tidy it up a bit.

Or the bee hives were put in there at the end of the oilseed season when the oil was about to be harvested and the hives might be in the way. But nothing had been in there recently, and the grass looked green and juicy.

'Perhaps it's for us,' said Marigold hopefully, but her hopes were dashed when a Land Rover and trailer turned into the yard. It was the same trailer that had brought Fat Pony.

'Not another pony,' exclaimed Marigold. 'Don't get me wrong Fat Pony, you're a very nice pony, but we don't need any more.'

'There weren't any more at the rescue place,' replied Fat Pony, but just then the ramp came down, the gates were opened, and 6 new arrivals trotted into the newly reinforced paddock.

'It's the goats,' cried Fat Pony with joy. 'Oh great. Come on Marigold, come and say hello. They're great fun.'

There were two very small goats, two golden goats and two goats with big noses and very long ears. 'Are they all goats?' asked Marigold dubiously. 'They all look very different. Two of them are no bigger than Patch. Are they babies?'

'No, they're the Pygmy goats, but do come and say hello.'

Marigold and Fat Pony moved along the fence to be nearer the goats and said a polite hello, as Farmer Fred shook hands with the man from the Land Rover, then waved him off.

'You've got some competition now Marigold old girl,' he said to the house cow. 'These produce milk as well.' Marigold looked them over and sniffed.

'You won't get much off those little ones,' she remarked. 'Not even enough for your morning cereal.'

One of the goats with long ears looked up. 'You're right,' she said. 'But they're here mainly for entertainment value. We Nubians and the Golden Guernseys do the milking.'

'Guernseys?' asked Marigold. 'Our families must have been near neighbours once. My family were from Jersey.'

One of the Guernseys came over for a proper sniff and hello, just as the two little goats started a game of hide and seek on the old dead tree trunk lying in their paddock.

'There you are,' said the floppy eared goat. 'I told you they were just for fun.'

Marigold and Fat Pony stood by the fence, laughing at the antics of the two tiny goats. First they jumped on and off the big old tree trunk in a mad game of follow my leader. Then they chased in and out of the long grass, ending with a flying jump back on to the tree trunk. One of them discovered that the sloping trunk was slippery and slid down it. The other one joined in, as the four bigger goats alternately watched and browsed. Then disaster struck!

One of the pygmy goats slid down the tree, jumped off into the long grass and caught her foot on a half-buried stone. She fell over with a cry and disappeared from view. Everyone turned to look, mouths open in horror, in Marigold's case with a big clump of grass hanging inelegantly out. Even Fat Pony stopped chewing to watch. The little goat reappeared, her head above the long grass, but she was limping.

'Oooo' she cried. 'That hurt. I think my leg may be broken.'

One of the Nubian's trotted up and sniffed the dangling leg. 'No, it's not,' she said briskly, 'any more than it was when you did the same thing yesterday. I suggest you are a bit more careful.'

Marigold heaved a sigh of relief. 'I can see these are going to be a laugh a minute.' she said.

Christmas at White Cows

Towards the end of December, when the schools had broken up for the winter holiday, Farmer Fred and Mrs Fred's granddaughter Liesl came for a visit. She had a great time walking round all her favourite places on the farm, admiring the new piglets, running away from Gertie Goose, and making the acquaintance of Marigold's new calf, Bluebell. On all her walks and visits she was, of course, accompanied by the loyal Scratchy Patch, bouncing along at her heels like a particularly animated shadow.

During the afternoon of Christmas Eve, Liesl hunted through her school bag, muttering to herself, then pulled an old, battered book out of the bag with an air of triumph.

'Got it,' she said, then looking at her grandma, getting very stressed and hot as she rolled out pastry for more mince pies, 'come on Patch. Let's go to the barn.'

As they crossed the yard, they saw Farmer Fred hiding in the cowshed. He knew better than to hang around in the kitchen when Mrs Fred was making mince pies. He whistled a carol as he shook fresh straw in with the calves. They bounced around and barked with excitement as they butted the new bales and threw the straw about. He waved, as Liesl pulled the big barn door open and went through. Inside it was warm, with scents of hay and the steamy breath of Marigold and Bluebell cudding peacefully. Liesl pulled up a bale of straw and sat down. Patch turned round and round on the hay strewn floor, and then she sat down too.

'Now Marigold, now Bluebell,' said Liesl. 'Please pay attention because I am going to read you a story.' And she read an old, old story about all the animals in a stable long ago, and how they watched as a tiny baby boy was born, and how they kept him warm with their hay scented breath as he lay asleep in their manger. She went on to explain how shepherds had brought their sheep to see the baby too; and that later in the night, they had all been surprised by a visit from some very grandly dressed travellers who had given the baby rich presents.

'And,' said Liesl as she concluded the story, 'ever since that day, on Christmas night, farm animals all over the world still kneel in memory of the special baby and the special night.'

She closed the book with a snap and turned to Marigold and Bluebell. 'I should like to see you tonight,' she said to the two Jersey cows, 'but I have to go home this afternoon. Happy Christmas to you both.'

After she had gone, Patch looked at Marigold. '*Do* you kneel on Christmas night?' she asked.

'Not that I know of,' said Marigold. 'I'm not exactly built for kneeling.' And she looked back along her comfortably rounded sides. 'It must have been a very special stable,' she said, 'and very crowded with all those sheep and travellers.'

That evening, the air was very still and cold. At midnight the moon was hidden below the horizon and just one star shone a clear white light down through the millions of miles to land at the doorway of the old barn. Marigold and Bluebell were standing together just inside the doorway, and the starlight silvered Marigold's horns. The old shire horse behind them rattled his headcollar just as the bell from the church steeple rang across the frosted fields. It was midnight.

Marigold looked at Bluebell, and then at Old Ben, the shire horse. Everywhere was quiet, except for the church bell. Even the geese by the pond and the sheep on the hill were quiet. As the bell struck 12, Marigold, Bluebell and Ben all bent their knees and sank to the ground to honour the Christ child.

ABOUT THE AUTHOR

Award-winning author Heather Peck has enjoyed a varied life. She has been both farmer and agricultural policy adviser, volunteer covid vaccinator and NHS Trust Chair. She bred sheep and alpacas, reared calves, broke ploughs, represented the UK in international negotiations, specialised in emergency response from Chernobyl to bird flu, managed controls over pesticides and GM crops, saw legislation through Parliament and got paid to eat Kit Kats while on secondment to Nestle Rowntree.

She lives in Norfolk with her partner Gary, two dogs, two cats, two hens and a female rabbit named Hero.

OTHER BOOKS

THE DCI GELDARD NORFOLK MYSTERIES

Secret Places

Glass Arrows *

Fires of Hate **

The Temenos Remains **

Dig Two Graves **

Beyond Closed Doors

Death on the Rhine (novella) **

Milestones (thriller)

BOOKS FOR CHILDREN

Tails of Two Spaniels **

The Pixie and the Bear

*shortlisted for the East Anglian Book Award prize for fiction 2021

**Firebird Book Award Winner